Dig In Deep

To Motivate and Inspire

JOSEPH T. HIPPARD

WestBow Press books may be ordered through booksellers or by contacting:

WestBow Press
A Division of Thomas Nelson & Zondervan
1663 Liberty Drive
Bloomington, IN 47403
www.westbowpress.com
844-714-3454

KJV: Scripture taken from the King James Version of the Bible.

ISBN: 978-1-6642-3600-4 (sc)
ISBN: 978-1-6642-3602-8 (hc)
ISBN: 978-1-6642-3601-1 (e)

Library of Congress Control Number: 2021910842

Print information available on the last page.

WestBow Press rev. date: 05/26/2021

WESTBOW
PRESS®
A DIVISION OF THOMAS NELSON
& ZONDERVAN

Dig In Deep

The first thing I want to say comes from the King James Version of the Holy Bible. Psalms chapter 82 verse 6 I have said, Ye are gods; and all of you are children of the most High. With that being said my god in the heaven just told me that I'm a god, meaning when I ask Jesus to help me with anything that I need that he's helping a god himself. Digging in deep I notice a nation of people who struggle with self-confidence and have low self-esteem. If you believe in god then that means that you should believe in yourself. It seems very depriving to think so low of oneself when the god in the heavens fancies you as a god. That is the most precious compliment that the Most High can give you to live a highly fulfilling life.

Equally important this is where we have to "Dig in Deep" being self-reliant in many trials of life. It pays off to stay motivated to get complicated task done. Unless you are a person who doesn't wish to leave a legacy behind you and you don't want to be remembered in the Era for which you live in today. If you don't like working then you can be a lazy god. Always moping around in depression, self-pity, and discouragement.

Despite this negative outlook we want to dig in deep for the things in our control. For the accomplishments and achievements that we want to have we have to be moved to action. A lot of things that we want to have are literally in reach. To reach them we have to stop talking about them and stop thinking about them. There is no talking or thinking where action is required. When you learn to look inside of yourself for what you need you'll find that it's already there.

Consequently you'll be the reaper of benefits and happiness once you've been moved to action. You have to take care of it. No one else will. It's up to you to make the choice. It's a small decision that everyone does not want to make. You have to move if you don't it will never get done. When I say this I'm speaking about the things in your mind that require action concerning you and only you.

As a matter of fact it is your job to chase greatness. In life we don't always get what we want, but we should learn something about ourselves from each new experience. Maybe there was a person who was of great interest to you who rejected you when you put up your petition. Instead of being unhappy about the rejection you should be happy that you had the strength to put up the proposal. You should be astounded about your ambitious campaign when it takes great courage to go after the things we feel as highly meaningful. These actions prove that you've evolved from the way you previously were. A lot of people don't know when they face rejection that they should give themselves a pat on the back for not failing to try.

In other words it's best to keep trying for our dreams. I don't like to play back burner to the things that I feel as highly meaningful to me. You shouldn't either. The mind is powerful as soon as you feel like giving up on something your mind discovers the grounds for breaking through an obstacle. You can't stop believing in yourself when great things take time. I love mistakes and rejection because they are learning tools to show you a better version of yourself. It's up to us to notice the lesson we are being taught concerning ourselves.

Deep down we have to recognize a unique power within ourselves. What is power? Power is the ability to do something or act in a particular way, especially as a faculty or quality. Power also is the capacity or ability to direct or influence the behavior of others or the course of events. What I want to do is to tap in to that unique power and enlighten others about that power. When you find your power then you find your purpose. This should cure the disease of low self-esteem and build your self-confidence concerning things that are important to you.

Moreover we have to be willing to change. We have to become different if we want to see new things go through. We might have to change our training behind the goal that we would like to reach. I never said we have to change the goal of being at the top. We might just have to change the method of the way that we're going to reach the top. Keeping your eyes open is vital to the goal being reached. The best learning can come from the senses. Being a good listener and observer can help you find new information. Attacking your weak spots can also be sniffing you out a future victory.

Believe it or not we have to set fire to the flames of passion behind our ambition. We must have a strong desire to do or achieve something, typically requiring determination and hard work. It will be unusually beyond you to not have a desire and determination to achieve success. Depending on what you want to achieve this success could be big or small, but the thing is it has to touch your ambitious nature. Today will never come again. When you feel weak, remember the things that made you strong.

Above all studying and praying both provide strength. Its one thing to pray about something you want to achieve but when you study and pray about it at the same time you'll receive tunnel vision focus. Using these two techniques with the proper motivation behind you will give you the tenacity to get the job done. Odds are, the people you admire have shown real tenacity in achieving their goals. Anything worth doing takes constant persistence, perseverance, and a hard headed determination. Tenacity is the quality of champions. Tenacity is displayed by someone who doesn't quit who keeps trying until they reach success.

Not to mention prayer is the most powerful weapon against trials. Believe in the power of prayer. If not for yourself, believe in it for others. The world is weak, prayer is powerful, and He can do anything. Don't study because you need to. Study because knowledge is power. Study because they can't take it away from you. Study because you want to know more. Study because it upgrades you. Study because you'll be rewarded with higher intelligence. You don't want to look back and know you could've done better.

In all probability, if you're brave enough to start, then you'll be strong enough to finish. Don't let others swindle your mind poisoning your self-confidence. Self-confidence is your superpower. Once you start to believe in yourself. Blessings begin to happen. Your success will be determined by your ambition and attitude. You will never regret reaching your goal. You will only regret giving up and not pushing beyond your limits.

For example you have to have an I will not be stopped mentality. Great things never come from our comfort zones. Circumstances don't have to stop you. If you get cornered don't turn around and give up. Figure out a way to get out. Move through it or work around it. You are only incarcerated by the chains you shackle yourself to. It's going to be hard to change yourself, but it's going to be worth it. I wouldn't want you to stop until you can say I am truly a champion. I am truly proud of myself. I made an impactful difference.

For the most part digging in deep is about finding the power within ourselves to act. Actions speak way louder than words. When your actions contradict what you are saying those words mean nothing. You have to create your happiness. Taking action will be the root of your success.

Notably, practicing self-control and maintaining one's self-esteem, goes hand and hand. Having self-control is power. Training to stay calm in difficult situations is smartness. You have to reach a place where your sacrifice doesn't change based off of you seeing someone else who won't sacrifice. Don't allow others to negatively influence your path to something better in life. Don't allow your emotions to overpower the power of positivity. To do this you must be disciplined like a soldier.

learn

If I'm not mistaken it would be a good idea to work in solitude and let your success reign in the public. I would be very mad at myself for giving up before the miracle came, because of all the days that I spent transforming myself in the darkness. Not knowing that victory was right around the corner.

To illustrate my point digging in deep is about the power to help others besides helping ourselves. Helping others is the way we help ourselves. A person's most useful asset is not a head full of knowledge, but a heart full of love, an ear ready to listen and a hand willing to help others. When you help others achieve you will achieve as well.

Furthermore beside those words of wisdom we really have to sit down and think about the things in life that will make us dig in deep. Which could be: getting the bills paid on time, helping your parents with the housing unit mortgage payments, paying off a college student loan, or getting that small business company started. Concerning these things that are of formal argument or logic. We might have to copy what army soldiers did. Which means zip up the zipper to the jacket and strap the boots up tight, because life will hand you a struggle that requires you to be a combat master. In defense of that you will have to dig in deep to bring out the willpower of a real beast. With that unique power you are going to have to utilize all your tools. Once you do that you can knock down Goliath with the spirit of David, and stand over your obstacles like a lion who is ruler with the queens of the jungle.

Studying

Train

Finally, gods and goddesses maneuvering the wheel to the boat which we call life, while living we have to be careful because we don't know how hard or when that storm can hit. We absolutely have to be attentive and prepared. The Most High gives his most precious compliments to us. There is a god inside of you. Dig in deep find it and make things happen. Make things change.

There are many reasons why we have to dig in deep to make things change. Others may suffer as a consequence of our inability to change. This might lead to separation from a group. The group of hard workers who work hard won't suffer any losses, but the loss of not acting will make us lose out on our dreams. To prevent this we have to be educated and aware of our why we must dig in deep. We must recognize the opportunity to be optimistic and avoid any situation that can lead to poverty.

About the Author

Joseph Hippard is an American book author who's first book is about inspiration and motivation. The Dig in Deep book was created to inspire and motivate you to dig in deep for goals and dreams that you may hope to accomplish in your near future. Teaching you to have strength and rely on yourself.

Printed in the United States
by Baker & Taylor Publisher Services